A Wisdom Retreat

30 Days of Spiritual Contemplation

with Stephen Davey

A Wisdom Retreat

Author: Stephen Davey

Editorial Team: Lalanne Barber, J. Seth Davey

Cover Design and Text Layout: Shannon Brown, Advanced Graphics (www.advancegraphics.us)

Day 1 - I Believe I Will

John 3:17-18

"For God did not send the Son into the world to judge the world, but that the world might be saved through Him. He who believes in Him is not judged; he who does not believe has been judged already, because he has not believed in the name of the only begotten Son of God."

I remember, as a boy, visiting the home of an elderly couple in Wisconsin as we traveled on our way to Minnesota. The man, in his eighties and near death's door, was confined to his chair. We sat in the living room—my father and mother, my three brothers, and I.

Although the man's children supported my missionary parents, he was not a Christian. I can still hear my father as he shared the plan of salvation with him and then asked, "Would you like to receive Christ as your own Savior? Would you like to ask Him into your life?"

The man said, "I don't believe I will."

Something pressed upon my father to risk offense, because he simply rewound his conversation and started over. He pulled his chair right up to the recliner where the old man was sitting wrapped in a comforter. I remember the urgency in my dad's voice.

Here was a man who had lived a respectable life, raised decent children, attended church, and accomplished a lot of good things. Here was my father telling him that he was *not* good enough in himself!

After explaining the gospel yet another time, Dad put the question to him again: "Would you now place your faith in Christ and simply receive Him as your personal Savior?"

I held my breath. It was then that the man replied, "I believe I will."

Now there were tears running down my cheeks. None of us knew it at the time, but within a few months the man would die.

Death comes to all. It's a reality of the planet we inhabit. This is the reason Jesus Christ came into the world—that it might be saved.

But why are we in this desperate condition? The Scriptures tell us that all men are sinners (*Romans 3:10-23*) and death is the result of that sin (*Genesis 2:17; Ephesians 2*). It is spiritual death.

Now that's a problem, and the solution can't be found in mankind because *all* men are dead. Christ took the punishment that was ours and bore it Himself, offering us His righteousness in return. He paid the debt for our sin on the cross. This He did for all who will believe and accept His gift of salvation.

The death, burial, and resurrection of the Savior provide the proverbial *life raft*, the *cure*, the *escape* from death's everlasting clutches. But the raft must be inflated; the cure must be swallowed; the escape must be made through the open door.

We would think it crazy that a drowning man would pass up a life raft and say, "I don't believe I'll get in it." It would be fatal to turn from the cure and say, "I don't believe I'll take it." It would be suicide to slam the escape door and say, "I don't believe I'll go." Yet, we seem quite unconcerned when a similar response comes from those with whom we've pled to accept Christ's love and sacrifice: "I don't believe I will."

How about you? As you start down this path of spiritual retreat, will you believe on His name and accept His shed blood as the payment for your sins? Will you receive His saving forgiveness? There should be only one answer . . . "I believe I will."

Prayer Point: If you have never come to know God through His Son, pray that He would show you the good news in John 3. If you do know Him, pray that God would help you keep in mind that *everyone* needs Jesus.

Extra Refreshment: Read Romans 3:21-26, the passage that some call the "heart of the Gospel."

Day 2 - Faith is . . .

Hebrews 11:1

Now faith is the assurance of things hoped for, the conviction of things not seen.

My favorite professor often quoted from Lewis Carroll's book entitled *Through the Looking-Glass*. He especially used the conversation between Alice and the White Queen:

"How old are you?" asked the queen.

"I'm seven and a half, exactly."

"You needn't say 'exactly'; I can believe it without that. Now I'll give *you* something to believe: I'm just one hundred and one, five months, and a day."

Alice protested, "I can't believe *that!*"

"Can't you? Try again—draw a long breath, and shut your eyes," the queen urged.

Alice roared, "There's no use trying; one can't believe impossible things!"

To this the queen responded, "I daresay you haven't had much practice. When I was your age, I always did it half-hour a day. Why, sometimes I've believed as many as six impossible things before breakfast."

The unregenerate man on Main Street, USA believes *this* is the meaning of faith: take a long breath, close your eyes, and begin to believe things that are *impossible* to believe.

What do you think? Maybe you have been afraid that this *is* its meaning. It is not!

We expect this kind of thinking outside the church, yet we are shocked when we find it *inside* the church. Faith is not an elusive, passive thing—it is *alive* and *active*.

The fruit of faith is substance and evidence—that which shows in our lives and proves what we believe.

So what is faith? Faith is the act of:

- considering Jesus Christ worthy of trust as to His character and motives;
- placing confidence in His ability to do just what He says He will do;
- entrusting the salvation of our soul into the hands of Christ;
- committing the work of saving our soul to the care of the Lord.

This means taking ourselves *out* of our own keeping and entrusting ourselves *into* the keeping of Jesus Christ.

This means that we listen to what God is saying in His Word. Paul exhorted Timothy, his son in the faith, to "accurately handle the word of truth" (*2 Timothy 2:15*) because it is "profitable for teaching, for reproof, for correction, for training in righteousness; so that the man of God may be adequate, equipped for every good work" (*2 Timothy 3:16-17*).

A friend once asked, "When was the last time God spoke to you and what did He say?" Then he held up his Bible and said, "This is where He is speaking. Are you hearing Him? Are you obeying Him?"

How about you—are you walking by faith? *"Now, faith is . . ."*

Prayer Point: Take time in your prayer life and Bible reading, treating it like a conversation. Before reading the Scriptures, ask God to help you *hear* Him. After reading the text, ask God to help you *obey* Him. Pray as the apostles said to the Lord, "Increase our faith!" *(Luke 17:5)*.

Extra Refreshment: Read in Hebrews 11 the instances of people hearing God and doing what He says.

Day 3 - Light Up the Runway!

Matthew 5:14-15

"You are the light of the world. A city set on a hill cannot be hidden; nor does anyone light a lamp and put it under a basket, but on the lampstand, and it gives light to all who are in the house."

James Dobson told a story about a friend who was flying his single-engine plane toward a small rural airport. When he arrived at the close of the day, the sun had already dropped behind the mountain. By the time he had maneuvered into position to land, he couldn't see the shadowy field below. There was no one on duty at the airport, and there were no lights on the plane

The pilot circled the runway for another attempted landing, but the darkness had become even more impenetrable. For two hours he flew around in the inky blackness, knowing full well that he faced certain death when his fuel tank emptied.

Then, as panic began to seize him, a wonderful thing happened. Someone who lived near the airport had heard the continuous drone of a small plane engine and realized there was a problem. That kind, merciful man raced to the airport and drove his car back and forth on the runway to indicate the direction of the airstrip. He then drove to the far end of the runway, positioned his lights, and turned them on high beam, to shine down the stretch of tarmac.

The pilot landed safely.

We all know the potential disaster that comes from being caught ill-equipped in darkness.

Maybe you drove to the restaurant anyway, even though your daughter reminded you that you don't see well enough to drive at night. Maybe you tried to get that last section of the deck stained before nightfall and discovered the streaks the next morning. Maybe you stepped on the only Lego left out on the floor as you started down the hallway to get a late-night drink of water.

Darkness can be frightening. Darkness can be dangerous. Darkness can be deadly.

But, "God, who said, 'Light shall shine out of darkness,' is the One who has shone in our hearts to give the Light of the knowledge of the glory of God in the face of Christ" (*2 Corinthians 4:6*).

This Light that He gave us is Himself. In John's Gospel, Jesus tells His disciples that He is the Light of the World (*John 8:12*). In the Sermon on the Mount in Matthew 5, Jesus Christ tells His disciples that *they* are the light of the world. This is to say that Christ puts His Light in us. This He does by giving us Himself.

Because God has given Himself to us, we in turn bear witness of God to others. What if the man who had illuminated the runway had decided to stay home?

The souls of the world hang in the balance, and without *Jesus Christ*, the Light of the World, they are destined to remain in the darkness—without God . . . without hope.

Grab your keys; start the engine; turn on the headlights—someone's in trouble. Don't make him circle the field again! Light up the runway . . . bring him in for a safe landing!

Prayer Point: Pray that God will give you opportunity to share Christ with others. Pray that you will have the courage to shine brightly.

Extra Refreshment: Read Luke 1:67-79 and experience the same joy as Zacharias in praising God for Jesus, the Light of the World.

Day 4 - Go to God

1 Samuel 1:10

She, greatly distressed, prayed to the LORD and wept bitterly.

If man had written the Bible without God's inspiration, he would have placed the people found there on pedestals and edited the script to remove all of their mistakes, sins, and failures. But God, the Master Artist, paints the heroes of the Bible with realistic brush strokes.

God records the whole story of these men and women—"warts" and all; He records their triumphs and also their tears. There are no perfect people parading across the pages of Scripture—there are *real* people with *real* problems.

There was an article in *Newsweek* written by a woman who had been the editor for a publisher producing self-help books. She wrote:

> You might expect that people who work for authors and bosses of such a company would, in general, be terribly well-adjusted folks—on a first name basis with all their feelings; bursting with self-esteem; free of type-A stress, phobias, and anxieties. Think again.
>
> The bosses are even now beginning construction on a second story for our building because the office manager and the head of typesetting cannot stand working in the same room together.
>
> One of the executive staff routinely gets so upset during phone calls that he falls out of his chair onto the floor.
>
> Two in-house authors of a book on stress are on the verge of suing each other.
>
> Our best-selling book on phobias and fears is lacking an author cover photo because—you guessed it—the author has a phobia about having his picture taken!

This is true not only in the secular world but in the sacred world as well. We are all made of clay! If anyone ever gives you the impression that he has it all together, you need to look again . . . or just quit looking.

Hannah was unable to have children; she also suffered the indignity of the mocking of her husband's other wife Peninnah, who was able to bear children. This added insult to injury! It would be unbiblical to say that Hannah, this great woman of faith, was not affected by this situation—she was miserable.

I Samuel 1:8-9 says, "Elkanah her husband said to her, 'Hannah, why do you weep and why do you not eat and why is your heart sad? Am I not better to you than ten sons?' Then Hannah rose after eating and drinking in Shiloh. Now Eli the priest was sitting on the seat by the doorpost of the temple of the LORD."

And here comes Hannah's flood of tears!

You may have had times like this: tears bathing your cheeks and washing your soul. But the wonderful thing in verse 10 is that Hannah poured out her soul to the Lord. She went *to* Him, not *away* from Him, in the time of her deepest sorrow.

Your heartaches are God's concern; your burdens are His to bear for you. You can take comfort in the knowledge that "casting all your anxiety on Him, because He cares for you," your heart will be eased *(1 Peter 5:7)*.

"God is our refuge and strength, a very present help in trouble" *(Psalm 46:1)*. Never forget that God is your greatest source of help; of strength; of comfort; of refuge.

What is it in your life that causes great distress? What causes you to weep bitterly? Whatever the reason, follow Hannah's example . . . go to God.

Prayer Point: Take time to pray to God, using *real* words about *real* things. Don't just utter the spiritual words that you think you should say—talk to your heavenly Father about your struggles; your feelings; your desires; your failures. Ask Him to help you trust His provision for your need.

Extra Refreshment: Read Hannah's prayer of exaltation in 1 Sam. 2:1-10, expressing her understanding of God's power.

Day 5 - Then Comes the Good Part!

John 20:18

Mary Magdalene came, announcing to the disciples, "I have seen the Lord," and that He had said these things to her.

A family was watching *The Greatest Story Ever Told*, a film on the life of Christ. One of the children in the family was deeply moved. As Jesus journeyed to Calvary, tears rolled down her cheeks. She sat absolutely silent until Jesus had been taken down from the cross and put into the tomb. Then she suddenly grinned and shouted excitedly, "Now comes the *good* part!"

Now comes the good part! Indeed it does! The resurrection of our Lord is the basis of our faith. Without it, we would be lost! Without the resurrection of Jesus Christ:

+ The gospel would be meaningless.

   . . . if you confess with your mouth Jesus as Lord, and believe in your heart that God raised Him from the dead, you shall be saved (Romans 10:9).

+ Forgiveness of sins would be hopeless.

   And if Christ has not been raised, your faith is worthless; you are still in your sins (1 Corinthians 15:17).

+ Present life would be joyless.

   Then those also who have fallen asleep in Christ have perished. If we have hoped in Christ in this life only, we are of all men most to be pitied (1 Corinthians 15:18-19).

+ Godly living would be fruitless.

   Truly, truly, I say to you, he who believes in Me, the works that I do shall he do also; and greater works than these shall he do; because I go to the Father (John 14:12).

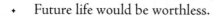

♦   Future life would be worthless.

> *Let not your heart be troubled; believe in God, believe also in Me. In My Father's house are many dwelling places; if it were not so, I would have told you; for I go to prepare a place for you* (John 14:1-2).

Do you understand what is at stake? If there is no resurrection, there is no Gospel; if there is no Gospel, there is no forgiveness of sin; if there is no forgiveness of sin, there is no present joy; if there is no present joy, there is no future hope.

We may sit silently during part of this life; we may shed abundant tears of sadness as we watch and wait. But just remember that Christ is preparing a place for us in His Father's house . . . and then comes the *good* part!

Prayer Point: Talk to the Lord with gratitude for your salvation. Use the words *death*, *burial*, and *resurrection* when you pray. Keep in mind that you have eternal life because of His resurrection.

Extra Refreshment: Read all of 1 Corinthians 15 for Paul's awesome teaching on the Resurrection.

Day 6 - God Uses Broken Things

John 21:15-17

So when they had finished breakfast, Jesus said to Simon Peter, "Simon, son of John, do you love Me more than these?" He said to Him, "Yes, Lord; You know that I love You." He said to him, "Tend My lambs." He said to him again a second time, "Simon, son of John, do you love Me?" He said to Him, "Yes, Lord; You know that I love You." He said to him, "Shepherd My sheep." He said to him the third time, "Simon, son of John, do you love Me?" Peter was grieved because He said to him the third time, "Do you love Me?" And he said to Him, "Lord, You know all things; You know that I love You." Jesus said to him, "Tend My sheep."

Kathy Ormsby was a success story: a dean's list student at North Carolina State University; a premed major; an All-American distance runner.

At the University of Pennsylvania Penn Relays in April, 1986 she set an American collegiate record for 10,000 meters. She was "on a roll," and qualified for the National Collegiate Athletic Association (NCAA) championships in 3000, 5000, and 10,000 meters. She was a celebrity, and everything seemed so right for this twenty-one-year-old junior in college.

But something was dangerously wrong—she had become obsessed with winning.

In the first week of June, 1986 she began the 10,000 meter run at the NCAA track championships in Indianapolis. At 6500 meters, she abruptly quit. Totally burned out, her life's purpose suddenly became clear: life was nothing more to her than just winning one more race.

She turned and jogged out of the stadium, ran to a bridge two blocks away, and jumped. She fell forty or fifty feet onto a flood plain.

Today this woman is paralyzed from the chest down. Kathy Ormsby will never run again. The *Seattle Times* article of June 11, 1986, asked the question, "How many other athletes, obsessed with winning, are heading for a fall?"

In today's text, Jesus Christ is restoring Peter from his denial and betrayal of Him. In loving mercy our Lord takes those who belong to Him—broken and despondent—and makes them whole and useful for His purposes.

This is the purpose of our lives: to know Him and to glorify Him. Paul called us "His workmanship, created in Christ Jesus for good works, which God prepared beforehand so that we would walk in them" (*Ephesians 2:10*).

Peter's difficulty stemmed from believing that he really was what his new name signified—a *rock*.

Jesus was in the process of teaching him an important concept: apart from His strength, Peter was a piece of crumbling sandstone. In other words, he was broken. That is painfully clear as Christ reverts to Peter's old name, asking, "Simon [*stone*] . . . do you love Me?"

Vance Havner wrote:

> "God uses broken things. It is the broken alabaster box that gives forth perfume. It is the broken soil that produces a crop; it is the broken clouds that give rain; it is the broken grain that gives bread, and it is the broken bread that gives strength. . . . God uses broken things."

Brokenness is defined as being totally subdued; humbled; weakened and infirmed; crushed by grief. It's not bad to find yourself in that condition; after all . . . God uses broken things.

Prayer Point: Lift your heart to God in surrender and submission, praying to be broken for His purposes. Tell Him you are willing to be changed!

Extra Refreshment: Read the letter to Philemon to get a perspective on a changed life.

Day 7 - The Church That Changed

Acts 11:1

*Now the apostles and the brethren who were throughout Judea heard that
the Gentiles also had received the word of God.*

I can still vividly remember a change that occurred in our household years
ago. It was when I took our older daughter to her first day of kindergarten.

If you had watched us from twenty yards away, we would have made the
perfect picture. She had on new shoes and was carrying her shiny lunchbox; I
was holding her hand as we walked from the parking lot to the school. But if
you had come within earshot, you would have discovered that we were actually arguing!

She wanted me to stay in the car, saying, "Daddy, I don't need you to take
me to class; I can do this by myself!" And I was saying, "Listen, you might be
feeling good about all this, young lady, but I'm not—so why don't you just allow
me a little insecurity! Okay?"

I remember that change. She went from a dependent five-year-old to an
independent kindergartener.

No change is easy. We naturally resist the rough waters; the upheaval; the
emotions; the hardships—there're all cousins to change.

The most difficult changes to make are those involving lifelong traditions
and heritage.

I'll be even more specific: changes are hard to accept when it comes to
church; when it involves your relationship to Christ; when it affects how you
worship.

How about you? Can you do an internal audit of your deeply cherished
church traditions?

Are they biblically based . . . or culturally based?

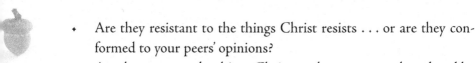

- ✦ Are they resistant to the things Christ resists . . . or are they conformed to your peers' opinions?
- ✦ Are they open to the things Christ teaches . . . or are they closed by personal bias?

Let's be honest: were the Lord to have restricted salvation to the Jews, we would be lost!

Since Israel is God's light to the nations, it was His predetermined plan that this light should shine to the Gentiles. Remember Abraham was given three promises from God in Genesis 12-17:

1. He would have the title deed to the land of Israel.
2. He would have a great progeny.
3. He would be a spiritual blessing to the entire world.

Paul asks in Romans 3:1, "What advantage has the Jew?" His answer was that they had the oracles [Word] of God, and Christ would be born of the natural seed of Abraham, thus fulfilling God's promise to him that he would bless the entire world.

So, what about us? Are we to be a blessing, too? Are we to accept, and even promote, change that brings the Gospel of Jesus Christ to all nations?

Are we to drop cultural barriers for the cause of Christ? Are we to welcome all who are saved into the family of God?

These questions bear answering . . . some traditions bear *changing*.

Prayer Point: Ask the Lord to give you a heart for people . . . and to help you see where change is needed in your own life. Most of all, ask Him to help you love others as Christ has loved you.

Extra Refreshment: Read Acts 15, and take note of the actions of the church when God worked among the Gentiles.

Day 8 - But You, O Lord ...

Psalm 102:11-12

My days are like a lengthened shadow, and I wither away like grass. But You, O Lord, abide forever, and Your name to all generations.

What you think these men had in common at the height of their careers during the 1930s, '40s, and '50s?

- Owen D. Young
- James F. Byrnes
- Pierre Laval
- Harlow Curtis
- Hugh Johnson

More than likely you do not recognize the names of any of these men. You certainly could not tell what they did or how they rose to fame. Yet each of these men was at some point in his life *Time Magazine*'s "Man of the Year." They were judged as the person having had the greatest impact on the rest of humanity during a given year.

It is our nature to think that we are really something special. This is why the business of *celebrity* is so successful. We have a desire to be great at something, and we are even willing to be somewhat satisfied with news of the lives of celebrities—reveling in their fame by proxy.

Think about the yearly audience of the Super Bowl; the Final Four; the NBA playoffs; the Masters; the Stanley Cup; Wimbledon; the Bowl games; the World Series. Factor in the weekly audiences of *American Idol; The Celebrity Apprentice; Survivor*, and many more "reality" shows. The American public has high hopes and watches intently to see who the winners will be.

Then you have the Academy Awards—for days before and after, water cooler talk centers on who will win/won which Oscar. Why? It's not as if the contenders are really the characters they portray—they're just good pretenders. Maybe that's why we find them so fascinating—we want to be good pretenders, too.

The writers of Psalms had no illusions about who we really are. There is line upon line in the book of Psalms regarding the nature of man.

Here in Psalm 102, the days of our lives are compared to withering grass, but not so the Lord's. He is great and His name lives for all generations—He is the same ... His years will have no end.

Why do we insist on plying mankind with glory and adulation when we have the God of the universe before us? Our attention and adoration should not be focused on man's folly, but rather upon the greatness of God. J. I. Packer addresses this very point:

> The Christian's instincts of trust and worship are stimulated very powerfully by knowledge of the greatness of God. But this is knowledge which Christians today largely lack; that is one reason why our faith is so feeble and our worship so flabby. We are modern men, and modern men—though they cherish great thoughts of man—have, as a rule, small thought of God.

Let's get real about ourselves and mankind as a whole: admit that underneath the façade the world sees, we all are sinners by nature, deserving *none* of mankind's praise.

Should we really care about the comings and goings [and every detail in between] of celebrities; stars; idols? *No!*

Let's focus our aim where it should be, and say with the Psalmist, "But You, O Lord ..."

Prayer Point: Ask the Lord to help you meditate on His greatness. As you read the Scriptures, take time to praise God for Himself—the One whose years will have no end.

Extra Refreshment: Read Psalm 103 and make the first and last verses come alive to you today.

Day 9 - "Not Guilty!"
Deuteronomy 31:6

Be strong and courageous, do not be afraid or tremble at them, for the Lord your God is the one who goes with you. He will not fail you or forsake you.

I have documentation from Rabbi Reuven Lauffer [Jerusalem, Israel] of an incredible story . . . one relating to the Holocaust: the incarceration and slaughter of Jews in the concentration camp known as Auschwitz. This true story took place toward the end of World War II.

At Auschwitz, as in all the camps, there was no lack of great Jewish scholars. One night ten of those learned men made up a Jewish court of law and put God on trial.

The central premise of the trial: how was it possible that God, who is totally good, could create such a living hell as Auschwitz? The debate raged back and forth all night; finally, the court returned a verdict of "Guilty!" God was guilty of failing His people.

However, upon adjourning the court, the entire barracks rose and began to pray their morning prayers. Even after finding God *guilty*, they prayed to Him!

What an incredible statement of faith it was for these Jews to continue praying to God, even while the torture and systematic killing continued. Yet, I thought how tragic that they were now praying to a God they believed had left them all alone.

If we were honest with ourselves, each of us could point to a time when we felt as though God had left us . . . and it took infinitely less than genocide to make us accuse God of abandonment.

When Moses gathers the people to hear his final counsel, he is 120 years old. His life drawing to a close and the final opportunity looming before him, Moses speaks to the Israelites, reminding them that God does not leave His children.

Think about it—they had just come from 400 years of generational slavery! They had not yet entered into the land which God had promised them!

A man's last speech is usually devoid of self-aggrandizement and is often saturated with words of truth. Moses spoke the words of our text; he believed—he *knew*—that God does not *ever* leave His children.

How did Moses convey this truth? He knew it in his heart; he professed it with his lips; he lived it until the end.

This marvelous promise of security should serve to strengthen us in the face of any and all trials. Our trust is in the Lord and His promises, as recorded in Scripture.

The words of the last verse from the great hymn "How Firm a Foundation" take on new meaning when we sing:

> *The soul that on Jesus hath leaned for repose*
> *I will not, I will not desert to his foes.*
> *That soul, though all hell*
> *Should endeavor to shake*
> *I'll never, no never, no never forsake.*

Do you cast your cares upon Jesus Christ (*1 Peter 5:7*) or charge that He isn't concerned? In the midst of your conflicts and struggles, do you trust and rest in God or indict, try, and find Him guilty of neglect?

Jesus said, "... lo, I am with you always, even to the end of the age" (*Matthew 28:20*).

Do you believe the words of Christ? If your answer is "Yes," then the verdict must be ... "*Not guilty!*"

***

Prayer Point: If you have had doubts about God's faithfulness, ask Him to increase your faith. Then ask Him to help you *remember* all that He has done for you and those whom you know and love. Take time to thank your trustworthy Father.

Extra Refreshment: Read and try to memorize 2 Timothy 2:11-13.

Day 10 - Invisibly Involved
Philippians 2:13

For it is God who is at work in you, both to will and to work for His good pleasure.

The internet has allowed people to engage in events worldwide. Today we can surf sites and witness incidents unfolding in real time.

A decade ago, much was made of the approaching millennium Y2K. At that time, an article from the *Wall Street Journal* caught my attention. Daystar International Ministry had high hopes of using a strategically located webcam to capture an unusual sight: the second coming of the Messiah! This was expected at the stroke of midnight, signaling the year 2000.

I won't take time to mention the prophetic problems Daystar was overlooking. Okay—maybe I *will* mention one . . . the people who care about His second coming won't be *watching* Him descend to Jerusalem; we'll be coming *with* Him!

Imagine capturing *God* on film! You would have Messiah where you could actually *see* Him. Your own personal DVD from Daystar for $29.99—if you purchase it in the next fifteen minutes, of course!

A paparazzi photo frenzy would be old news compared to such a spectacle as this.

A miraculous sighting of the Lord seems far more marketable and exciting than the invisible working of God . . . an idea that won't sell many DVDs.

Still, the longing in all our hearts remains—a longing that has television shows spinning off series after series: trying to understand the ways of God; imagining how heaven responds to earth; interpreting the role of angels and demons in the affairs of mankind.

There are today fabricated reports of miraculous occurrences all across the globe: visions, sightings, miracles, and strange happenings.

I'll admit that it would be exciting to see with my own eyes a miracle performed by God. That's so much more interesting than attempting to discern

His invisible providence—His invisible working in the ordinary events of everyday life.

Yet for the believer today, that is where God actually *is* at work—in the mundane, tiring, ordinary, and even repetitive duties of life. It may come without the thunder and lightning of Mount Sinai, but He is working in our lives right now just as He worked in the lives of His disciples and followers in the first century.

Howie Stevenson, former Music Minister who served with Pastor Chuck Swindoll for many years, was fond of saying, "God moves among the casseroles." He meant that God was just as much at work in a person making dinner in the kitchen as He was in Paul planting a church in Ephesus.

God knows how easy it is for you to doubt His sovereignty when you don't see and hear His power . . . or sense His presence in the silence. But He *has* spoken, and He *is* present.

Walter Chalmers Smith put it this way when he wrote the first verse to a hymn in 1867:

> Immortal, invisible, God only wise,
> In light inaccessible hid from our eyes,
> Most blessed, most glorious,
> The Ancient of Days,
> Almighty, victorious—
> Thy great name we praise.

Kitchens, cubicles, car pools, and conference rooms—all are the Holy of Holies. You are in His presence today; although invisible, He is at work in you at this very moment. You don't need a camera to prove it—God *promised* it.

So trust His heart . . . even when you can't see His hand.

Prayer Point: Ask the Lord for greater trust in His presence and involvement in your life, addressing Him as "The God of Abraham, Isaac, Jacob, and *me*." This will help remind you that He is the God of all history—past *and* present.

Extra Refreshment: Read 2 Corinthians 1:2-7 to see one way that God is absolutely involved in your life.

Day 11 - The One Left Standing

Esther 3:2

All the king's servants who were at the king's gate bowed down and paid homage to Haman; for so the king had commanded concerning him. But Mordecai neither bowed down nor paid homage.

The book of Esther is a fascinating story of God's preservation of His people Israel. One of the great characters in that account is Queen Esther's uncle Mordecai. When one of the king's officials demanded that all bow down to Haman, Mordecai would not. When asked why, he simply stated that he was a Jew.

There is a price to pay when we take a stand, and those standing for Jesus Christ most often are called to make the greatest sacrifice. God wrote the book on standing alone—and He is the One who can help us through it.

This testimony during Hitler's reign of terror is from Erwin Lutzer's book *Hitler's Cross*:

> In June 1937, Dr. Niemoller preached his last sermon during the days of the Third Reich. He said to his congregation, "We have no more thought of using our own powers to escape the authorities than the Apostles of old. No more are we ready to keep silent at man's request when God commands us to speak. For it is, and must remain, the case that we must obey God rather than man."
>
> Within a few days, he was arrested and imprisoned. His trial began on February 7, 1938. During the previous seven months, he had been in solitary confinement. The indictments against him comprised fourteen pages. He was accused of speaking against the Reich with malicious and provocative criticism. He had violated the law, thus charged with "Abuse of Pulpit." In his biography *Pastor Niemoller*, Deitmar Schmidt tells the story of how a green-uniformed official

escorted Niemoller from his prison cell to the courtroom. Alone with his escort he walked, filled with dread and loneliness. Niemoller knew that the outcome of the proceedings was a foregone conclusion. Where were his family and friends? Where was his church, which had stood with him?

At that moment, he had one of the most uplifting experiences of his life. His escort had, so far, not uttered a word, but walked with regular footsteps, his face impassive. As they passed through the underground tunnel and were about to walk up the last flight of stairs, Niemoller heard a voice repeating a set of words. It was so low that it was difficult to know where it was coming from because of the echo. Then he realized it was his escort repeating, *"The name of the Lord is a strong tower; the righteous runs into it and is safe"* (Proverbs 18:10).

Niemoller was climbing the steps by now and gave no sign that he had heard the words. But his fear was gone, and in its place was the calm brilliance of an utter trust in God.

You can have that same trust today. Turn to the One who is your refuge; the One who can be touched with the feelings of your infirmities; the One who was tested in all points, as you are.

Fixing our eyes on Jesus, the author and perfecter of faith, who for the joy set before Him, endured the cross . . . (Hebrews 12:2).

While the world is desperately calling us to bow down to people and things other than God, determine that you will not; you can be the one left standing . . . for now and eternity.

Prayer Point: Pray for strength and trust to stand for Christ . . . *alone*, if need be.

Extra Refreshment: Read Esther 3-8 for "the rest of the story."

Day 12 - Imitating Christ
1 Corinthians 11:1

Be imitators of me, just as I also am of Christ.

Sometimes I stay up late to watch television—the second half of a football game; the NBA playoffs; a comedian. One of my favorite types of comedy is impersonation.

To be a really good impersonator, you have to essentially mimic the gestures, voice, and even the appearance of the one being imitated. To be successful in that field, I imagine you would have to spend a lot of time choosing a character and diligently developing the attributes necessary to impersonate him/her.

That thought triggered another, and I realized that I had observed an interesting pattern in my studies, both of Bible characters and the humans who live on this planet: to be an effective Christian, we must imitate the right people.

Scripture is filled with godly examples—the Apostle Paul, among others.

While in Philippi, Paul writes to the church at Corinth. In his letters he models the behavior for those who follow Jesus Christ. Two statements in particular stand out as he sums up his thoughts to the Corinthian believers:

+ *Whether, then, you eat or drink or whatever you do, do all to the glory of God* (1 Corinthians 10:31).

+ *Be imitators of me, just as I also am of Christ* (1 Corinthians 11:1).

The Apostle Peter writes to the strangers [believers] who were scattered abroad, and reminds them whom they were to follow:

For you have been called for this purpose, since Christ also suffered for you, leaving you an example for you to follow in His steps (1 Peter 2:21).

Paul pens instructions regarding the demeanor of believers. He writes this to the church at Philippi while he is imprisoned in Rome:

Have this attitude in yourselves which was also in Christ Jesus, who, although He existed in the form of God, did not regard equality with God

a thing to be grasped, but emptied Himself, taking the form of a bond-servant, and being made in the likeness of men. Being found in appearance as a man, He humbled Himself by becoming obedient to the point of death, even death on a cross (Philippians 2:5-8).

Again—while in chains at Rome—Paul urges the believers in Colosse regarding their actions:

Therefore as you have received Christ Jesus the Lord, so walk in Him (Colossians 2:6).

The greatest example set for us is our Savior, Jesus Christ. Matthew tells us in Christ's own words that sacrifices are required when we imitate God's Son:

"And he who does not take his cross and follow after Me is not worthy of Me" (Matthew 10:38).

The real secret of successful imitation is found through an intense study of the person, observing the character of the one whom we seek to imitate. Thus, as we follow after Christ, Paul encourages us with these words:

But we all, with unveiled face, beholding as in a mirror the glory of the Lord, are being transformed into the same image from glory to glory . . . (2 Corinthians 3:18).

The ultimate compliment to our Master is to become so like Him that it would be second nature to us. That can only happen when we walk with Him . . . in His steps.

Prayer Point: Pray that God would help you to study diligently, developing characteristics that reflect His influence in your life. Also, ask God to help you be worthy of imitation as an example for another believer, as you follow in His steps.

Extra Refreshment: Think about John the Baptist's statement in John 3:30 and how it would help as you seek to become an example to others.

Day 13 - People of the Word
Ezra 7:10

For Ezra had set his heart to study the law of the Lord *and to practice it, and to teach His statutes and ordinances in Israel.*

How many hours in the past week did you spend:

+ reading the newspaper?
+ watching television; DVDs; movies?
+ enjoying other forms of entertainment?
+ working on a hobby?
+ reading and studying the Bible?

Now we could argue the value of hobbies, movies, play-off games, newspapers—and never really get anywhere. I'm not suggesting that any of these things are wrong. My argument isn't along the lines of the inherent value in any one category; my concern has to do with the time they demand and the influence they exert in our lives.

Is it any wonder that the average Christian today knows a lot more about the world but much less about the Word?

+ We discuss events in Europe and the Middle East but aren't conversant about Colossians and the Minor Prophets.
+ We identify fads and fashion but cannot define our faith.
+ We dabble in the philosophy of the world but ignore the theology of the Word.
+ We defend our political preferences but cannot defend the Gospel.
+ We quote stock prices but cannot quote Scripture.
+ We know the most popular actors and recording artists by name but don't know the books of the Bible by heart.
+ We find our way through *The Wall Street Journal* and *Fortune* magazine but can't locate the Ten Commandments or the Sermon on the Mount.

Are we people of the *world* or are we people of the *Word*?

Along with the Jews who returned from the Babylonian captivity, the godly priest Ezra had been allowed to lead the way in rebuilding the city of Jerusalem. However, Ezra recognized that much more was needed in the hearts of the people than homes and secure walls around their city. *"For he set in his heart to study the law of the LORD and to practice it, and to teach His statutes and ordinances in Israel"* (Ezra 7:10).

So wise Ezra included in the building project the most important foundation of all—the Scriptures. He knew that this underpinning alone would provide the best footing for the people to take a godly stand in life. He realized that this bedrock alone would allow the people of God to truly rebuild their broken lives.

This is the power and purpose of the Word of God: bread to eat *(Deuteronomy 8:3)*; light to see *(Psalm 118:105)*; our delight and meditation *(Psalm 1:2)*; all profitable direction and equipping for every need *(2 Timothy 3:16)*. This was their foundation—and yours! The Bible remains *the* manual for genuine faith and godly living.

I recommend that you join the commitment of the people of Israel: when returning to Jerusalem, they learned that of all the things they built, the most important was their lives . . . built upon and infused with the Word of God.

And remember, you will never have a close relationship with God if you have a distant relationship with His Word. So begin reading—and memorizing it . . . *today*!

Prayer Point: Ask God to give you a fervent hunger for His Word. Ask Him to make you dissatisfied with looking elsewhere for life's answers.

Extra Refreshment: Read Matthew 4:1-11, the account of Jesus' wilderness temptation. Look up His responses to the devil's offers and read them in their full context. Could you stand against temptation if you had to rely solely upon your understanding and recall of Scripture? Start equipping yourself today!

Day 14 - The Good Shepherd

Psalm 23

The LORD is my shepherd, I shall not want. He makes me lie down in green pastures; He leads me beside quiet waters. He restores my soul; He guides me in the paths of righteousness for His name's sake. Even though I walk through the valley of the shadow of death, I fear no evil; for You are with me; Your rod and Your staff, they comfort me. You prepare a table before me in the presence of my enemies; You have anointed my head with oil; my cup overflows. Surely goodness and lovingkindness will follow me all the days of my life. And I will dwell in the house of the LORD forever.

A modern-day shepherd was tending his sheep at the edge of a country road.

A new Jeep Grand Cherokee screeched to a halt beside him. The driver—dressed in a designer suit, expensive shoes, flashy wristwatch, and sunglasses—asked the shepherd, "Say, if I can guess how many sheep you have, will you give me one of them?"

The shepherd looked at the man, sizing him up, then looked at his flock grazing on several hundred acres around him and said, "All right."

The young executive parked his SUV, connected his notebook and wireless modem, entered a NASA site, scanned the ground using his GPS, opened a data base, and then printed a report from his portable laser printer. He walked over to the shepherd and said, "You have exactly 1,586 sheep in your flock."

The shepherd answered, "I can't believe it—you're right. Wow! Okay, take your pick . . ."

The young man took one of the animals, lifting it into the back of his Jeep. Then, just as he was about to drive away, the shepherd called out to him, "Hey, wait! Before you leave—if I can guess your profession, will you repay me?"

The executive answered with a smirk, "Sure, go ahead and try."

The shepherd said, "You're a consultant."

The man was shocked! With surprise written all over his face he conceded, "That's right . . . but how in the world did you know?"

The shepherd responded, "Very simple. First you came here to tell me something without being invited. Second, you charged me for information I already knew. Third, you really don't know anything about *my* business and . . . I'd really like to have my *dog* back!"

I wonder—is it possible that we know so little about our wonderful Shepherd because, like that businessman, we know very little about sheep?

Our Lord, the Good Shepherd, knows *His* business; furthermore, He is masterful at His care for the sheep. In this well-known Psalm, David considered himself to be a member of God's flock. And because David knew what the life of sheep was like, he penned this poem with their benefits in mind—benefits only possible when the Lord is our Shepherd:

1. He provides green pasture—not a coincidence in the Middle East, but the result of hard work.

2. Lying down in green pasture implied the lack of fear—sheep will stay standing unless they are secure in their shepherd's care.

3. He provides still water: inlets dug from a river since sheep are too timid to drink from running water.

4. He anoints the heads of sheep plagued with flies. The ointment provides soothing relief from the irritations of life—soothing only from a personal relationship between sheep and shepherd . . . and that's just the beginning!

Prayer Point: Ask God to help you see Him as a caring, nurturing Shepherd. Thank Him for His dependability and provision.

Extra Refreshment: Read John 10:1-30 for Jesus Christ's perspective on the Good Shepherd.

Day 15 - Truly Good News
Romans 1:16-17

For I am not ashamed of the gospel, for it is the power of God for salvation to everyone who believes, to the Jew first and also to the Greek. For in it the righteousness of God is revealed from faith to faith; as it is written, "But the righteous man shall live by faith."

Several years ago I was in the waiting area of a Hindu temple in India and noticed a plaque on the wall. It had a message declaring how someone could find eternal life:

> He who desires to cross the painful ocean of worldly life, which is full of the crocodiles of anger, greed, and infatuation, should catch hold of the Bhagavad Gita which has the disciplines of action, devotion, and wisdom as its oars. It will easily take him to the land of liberation.

This is the Hindu path to heaven, or *Nirvana*. This is their "gospel." By the way, Hinduism requires that every person must spend time in one of twenty-one hells that burn away bad karma. Once purged, the soul is recycled to a higher state in the next life and the cycle begins again. If someone has been particularly bad in the previous life, he might be condemned to one of the lowest hells, where he will be cooked in jars or eaten by ravens! How's that for "good news"?!

For those who pursue Buddhism—well, it's not much easier to reach the Promised Land. Buddhism has its seven hot hells, complete with torture chambers and quagmire. There are also eight *cold* hells for those guilty of *lesser* sins.

Catholicism requires that confessions be made to priests; penances be purchased; last rites be performed. Catholics dread a future Purgatory where they undergo fires of purging for thousands of years before being allowed into heaven. From Pope to common parishioner, everyone must suffer the fires of

torment and be purged—hopefully living a life good enough to limit his "sentence" in Purgatory.

Frankly, all the man-made religions of the world are flawed in their teachings. They really don't have any Good News.

Every false religious system may not threaten believers with being cooked in jars or frozen in a cold hell, but they are equally hopeless in their systems of self-improvement.

Mankind intuitively knows that we have a "sin problem." Without any catechism lessons, everyone understands the concepts of sin and guilt. God has written His law on every man's heart.

Because of that instinctive knowledge, the human race is yearning for good news. That's what the word "Gospel" means—*good news*.

Paul wrote that the Gospel of Christ is the power of God for salvation for everyone who believes. The Gospel is the solution to mankind's sin. The Gospel is where the righteousness of God is offered to those who recognize they have no other hope or help.

The Gospel is an invitation to cling to the One who already suffered for our sins on the cross—not to our own ability to suffer for our sins until they are purged.

On another journey to India, I made video footage of a Hindu priest washing in the polluted waters of the Ganges River. He believed this ritual would wash his sin away. It struck me that both physically and spiritually, he was dirtier after he came out of the river!

Remember God's righteousness through His Son's atoning sacrifice for our sin; it's the only good news . . . *truly* good news.

Prayer Point: Thank God for His true Gospel: Christ's death was our full and final payment for sin. If you never have, ask Christ to save you.

Extra Refreshment: Read Romans 1:1-3:20 to grasp the fullest picture of mankind's sin problem. Then read Romans 3:21-26 for God's miraculous solution—the *good news*.

Day 16 - The *Stops* of a Good Man

Proverbs 4:26-27

Watch the path of your feet and all your ways will be established. Do not turn to the right nor to the left; turn your foot from evil.

Three young men from Tampa FL were driving home one evening after finishing a night of bowling. Kevin was driving his white Camaro, his friend Brian was riding in the front passenger seat, and Randall was sitting in the back. They drove through a familiar intersection, unaware of the danger that awaited them. Kevin didn't notice that the stop sign was missing from this busy intersection. He never even slowed down.

He assumed the other car would stop . . . it didn't (that stop sign was missing, too). The two cars collided; Kevin, Brian, and Randall were instantly killed.

An investigation eventually led to discovering the young men who were responsible for this tragic accident. They confessed to stealing the stop sign. It was just a prank. In fact, they admitted to stealing other stop signs in the area and dumping them into the river on the outskirts of town.

Who would be reckless enough to steal a stop sign?

Apparently, stealing road signs is a fairly popular prank these days. In the state of Texas alone, 50,000 road signs are vandalized every year—costing the state more than $2,000,000! But two million dollars can't compare to the lives of three men. The cost of those lives is priceless.

I can't help but think of the analogy to our culture today. It seems that wherever God puts up a stop sign, someone comes along and takes it down.

It's just fun to do. Besides, stop signs mean *rules*—laws—and no one likes either . . . they slow you down.

What a dangerous game to play. Pulling down God-ordained stop signs is a setup for disaster.

Christians are not immune to tragic collisions. Even believers ignore the fact that God has given us stop signs to *help* us rather than *harm* us. They are for our spiritual protection, safety, and security.

God isn't interested in creating a bunch of rules because He's some kind of cosmic killjoy, but our society would have us think that.

God actually sees the headlights of an oncoming car; He's fully aware of dangerous intersections; He protects us by clearly revealing His wisely ordained stop signs along the road of life.

Are you surrendered to the Lord's direction for your life? This includes both *steps* and *stops*!

What are some of the signs that you might be tempted to ignore today . . . or to remove?

Perhaps a friend is warning you to slow down or stop; Scripture jumps out at you, highlighting the verses on the danger of dating an unbeliever; the Holy Spirit persistently whispers a warning regarding dangerous activities: online surfing . . . boardroom compromising . . . expense account fudging.

Whatever form God's stop signs take, learn to obey them . . . stop signs are there to save your life!

Prayer Point: Would you let the Lord examine your heart today and convict you of any hidden sins you might be holding on to? Ask Him to give you eyes to see beyond the here-and-now—eyes that look into the future to see where your decisions might be leading you. Then pray for wisdom to make courageous decisions, knowing that God has promised to give you the strength to slow down—or maybe even stop—at just the right time.

Extra Refreshment: Read all of Proverbs 4, where Solomon tells his son to watch out for some very important stop signs.

Day 17 - Down Memory Lane

1 Chronicles 16:11-12

Seek the Lord and His strength; seek His face continually. Remember His wonderful deeds which He has done; His marvels and the judgments from His mouth.

Some of you had the privilege of living in one house throughout your entire childhood. It is a rare occasion these days, but I was fortunate enough to have lived in the same home for 18 years before I went to college.

During my freshman year, my parents moved. They were kind enough to send me their new address!

A few years ago I decided to take a trip down memory lane and see that old house where I had grown up. I climbed the steps to that familiar porch and knocked on the door, hoping that whoever lived there would let me revisit the rooms freighted with meaning and memories.

A young woman carrying a baby on her hip answered the door. I said, "I know this is going to sound strange, but I grew up in this house. I lived here 25 years ago and I'd love to walk through it again." She said, "Cool! C'mon in," and I did.

I walked into the living room with my shoes on. That was a *no-no* when I was growing up, and I half expected to hear my mother's reminder coming from the kitchen for me to leave my dirty shoes at the door!

I turned right and made my way into the dining room. I noticed the drop ceiling that my father had hung many years before was still in place.

From there I moved into the kitchen and peered through the familiar side door that overlooked the back yard. I noticed that the infamous bush was gone: that bush had supplied my mother with an ample amount of switches for four mischievous sons. The *bush* was gone. God had answered my prayers at last— decades later!

I finally made my way upstairs to my little bedroom. This was by far the most endearing place of all. To my left was open floor space, long ago occupied by my bed. That was where I had knelt one night as a teenager and gave my heart and my life—without reservation—to Jesus Christ. That was the place where it all started for me—it was the place where my spiritual life began.

There's something special about taking trips down memory lane, isn't there? Whether it's visiting an old home or catching up with a friend you haven't seen in years. It seems that as soon as you step through the door or see the face of that loved one, things just pick up right where they left off. Memories have a way of flooding back as old times are relived through laughter and tears.

Have you found the same to be true in your relationship with God? One of my professors in college once said to me that the Christian life isn't so much about learning *new* things about God as it is remembering the *old* things. God has done so much for us in the past and, like that old hymn so beautifully confirms, "He's proved His love o'er and o'er."

Our problem is that we often forget what God has done. As days turn to months and months to years, bringing new trials and new challenges, we forget to retrace our steps of faith and remember how God provided in every circumstance.

We're so focused on the present that we forget to visit the past.

Perhaps you need to reminisce today . . . to ponder the events where God was with you and brought you safely through the troubled waters to the other side.

When your future seems dark and discouraging, perhaps the best muscle to exercise is your memory. Do what David urged the Israelites to do in 1 Chronicles 16 . . . take a trip down memory lane!

Prayer Point: Take some time to write down specific instances where God has proven Himself to you in a powerful way. Then praise Him for His unfailing love which stays with us even when we forget it's there.

Extra Refreshment: Read 1 Chronicles 16:1-36, recounting where David pleads with the Israelites to remember God's character and covenant promises. Israel needed reminding as much as we do.

Day 18 - Walking in the Spirit

Romans 8:3-4

For what the Law could not do, weak as it was through the flesh, God did: sending His own Son in the likeness of sinful flesh and as an offering for sin . . . so that the requirement of the Law might be fulfilled in us, who do not walk according to the flesh but according to the Spirit.

Did you notice that the verse you just read is all about God and not about us? Simply paraphrased, Paul is saying, "For what *we* through the Law could not do . . ."

Everything from salvation to sanctification to future glorification is all a work of God's Spirit on our behalf.

This is another way of saying that people who "walk in the Spirit" are not people who have everything figured out. They are merely people who rely on God's strength, one step at a time.

I have a friend whose testimony illustrates this point very well. Before he became a believer, he was sentenced to four years for "white-collar crimes." But God would use his imprisonment to bring spiritual freedom.

Early into his incarceration, he was on the phone with his sister who shared the gospel with him. He broke into tears and prayed to receive Christ as His Savior. His life would change dramatically from that point.

His first night as a Christian, he began reading a Bible that a friend had given him. A fellow inmate saw him reading and asked him if he wanted to start a Bible study. He thought that was a great idea, but he didn't want to be in charge of leading it; besides, he was a brand-new believer and didn't know much about the Bible.

Nevertheless, after dinner that night, my friend made his way to the Bible study. When he arrived, the same inmate slipped an "Our Daily Bread" devotional into his hand and asked him to read it. Many of the men in the Bible

study couldn't read or write, so he began to read aloud. That particular devotional was all about giving your heart to Jesus Christ. When he finished reading several men said, "We want to do that . . . but how do we do it?"

He wasn't quite sure what to say. And at that very moment, he was paged to come to the office wing of the prison. As he walked there he prayed, "Lord, help me provide an answer to these inmates who want to know You personally."

On his way back, an inmate standing nearby reached out and handed him a bookmark and said, "You might want to read this sometime." The bookmark was entitled "How to Be Saved," and it clearly outlined the steps and verses of Scripture for accepting Christ as Lord and Savior.

Suddenly equipped with exactly what he needed, he walked back to the Bible study and read each step on that little bookmark from "Admit you are a sinner," to "Ask Christ to be your Savior." Four inmates prayed to receive Christ that night!

When this newly converted inmate had a problem . . . God was ready with His provision.

It is little wonder that to this day, now released from prison, my friend continues to share the gospel of Christ with anyone who will listen.

Let's learn from his experience. Walking according to the Spirit is as much a work of God as becoming a Christian or leading someone else to faith in Christ.

When we, like this inmate, admit our helplessness to God, He accomplishes His desires, for His glory alone, in us and through us.

And His provision will always be just what we need, when we need it most. It might not be anything all that special to anyone else, but to us it will be unmistakable evidence that we are walking in the Spirit . . . even if it's nothing more than a little bookmark!

Prayer Point: Let's pray the simple but effective prayer that Charlie prayed: "Holy Spirit, work with me here!" But only pray for God's help if you're really ready for Him to use you . . . because He will!

Extra Refreshment: Read Romans 8.

Day 19 - The Dreaded Word: *Practice!*

Hebrews 5:14

But solid food is for the mature, who, because of practice, have their senses trained to discern good and evil.

When I was just a boy, my parents made me practice at the piano for an hour a day. Was that cruel or *what?* I took piano lessons from the 2nd grade until I entered the 11th grade. In my senior year I tied for first place in a national competition with an original piece in G minor entitled *Summer's End.*

When I went to college I thought it would be a good idea to continue taking lessons. So I asked around to see who was considered the best piano teacher on the music faculty. Every person I asked gave the same name: Mrs. Hermann. This woman was so well-respected for her musical expertise that the college music hall had already been named after her and her husband.

Well, that settled it. I went to Mrs. Hermann's studio and knocked on her door. She came to the door and I said, "Mrs. Hermann, I'd like to take piano lessons from you."

She replied, "I'm sorry, but my schedule is now full."

I begged, "Please, I've been told you're the best teacher on campus . . . would you let me play something for you first?"

She agreed. I went in, sat down at the piano, and played for about a minute before she interrupted me and said, "I'll make room for you on my schedule." "Great!" I said, rather proud of myself for making such a good impression.

She then said, "Now you need to understand that if you take lessons from me you will be expected to practice four hours." I said, "No sweat! Four hours a week will work just fine!"

She then replied, "No, young man—I mean four hours every *day!*"

Whoa! In that moment, my entire life passed before my eyes. I couldn't imagine any torture greater than practicing that much. With a polite handshake, Mrs. Hermann and I parted ways and I decided then and there that becoming a better pianist wasn't that important after all!

As I look back on that decisive moment, not to mention the 10 years of piano lessons that preceded it, I've come to realize that learning to play the piano has a lot in common with learning to live the Christian life. The same concept applies to both: if you want to achieve a higher level of performance, you have to be willing to practice.

Salvation is a gift . . . spiritual discernment isn't. Salvation can happen in a moment; spiritual maturity takes a lifetime. In fact, having a discerning, godly walk with Christ will require hours of practice every day. That's why the writer of Hebrews reminded his audience that the ability to discern between good and evil is only acquired through consistent practice.

But this is an encouraging message to us. We can start at any time. Wherever you find yourself today, whether just a beginner in the Christian life or a believer for many years, start practicing. And keep in mind that Jesus Christ is the only One who ever mastered the Christian life. He also happens to be both the Model and the Teacher of how to walk in wisdom.

Thankfully, He always has room in His schedule to teach one more student. But He's a lot like Mrs. Hermann: He expects His students to practice. And the students who learn and grow in godly discernment are always the ones who are willing to practice . . . every single day.

Prayer Point: Identify areas in your life where you have grown over the past few months and thank God for giving you strength to change. Then identify areas where growth is still needed; pray for God's strength to help you change over time.

Extra Refreshment: Read Psalm 15, which outlines for us the attributes we as Christians should incorporate into our lives.

Day 20 - Putting on the Dog
Ephesians 4:22-24

You were taught with regard to the former way of life to put off the old self, which is being corrupted by its deceitful desires; to be made new in the attitude of your minds; and to put on the new self, created to be like God in true righteousness and holiness.

For centuries the aristocracy of Europe showed off their wealth in a number of pretentious ways. Not only did they live in mansions and travel in ornate coaches, but upper-class women spent lavish amounts of money to have small dogs bred. They were referred to as "lap dogs" and became as much a part of the fashion of the day as the expensive gowns worn by the elite.

Over time, it became a trademark of the wealthy for a woman to have her portrait painted with a little dog nestled in her lap.

In America, the late 1800s brought times of financial prosperity for many people. Men became millionaires almost overnight through the development of the railroad, oil, and real estate. Many of the wives of these businessmen desired to emulate their wealthy counterparts in Europe and not to be outdone, they acquired lap dogs of their own, spending large amounts of money in the process. One of the most popular dogs bred and owned during this time was the poodle.

Cynical observers took notice of this practice and coined the phrase, "putting on the dog"—a phrase which still exists today, meaning ostentatious activity by someone who is attempting to show off his/her wealth or position in society.

Unfortunately, this same principle is carried over into our churches every Sunday morning. We put on the dog more often than we would like to admit . . . and in more ways than perhaps we even know.

Consider these examples: faking a pious attitude in the service when our hearts are far from sincere; flaunting our clothing or accessories in an unseemly way; using spiritual vocabulary to make people think better of us than we

deserve; making an exaggerated display of dropping the gift in the offering plate—the list goes on.

Pretentiousness takes many different forms and we all struggle with it in our lives.

Frankly, it's a lot more comfortable to put on the dog than it is to expose who we really are. Transparency is extremely difficult, and sometimes it's just easier to hide behind a poodle!

But while everyone else might be fooled into thinking that we have it all fluffed up and under control, God sees past the makeup, the expensive suit, and the bleached smile.

God sees our hearts and knows exactly who we are at any moment. God sees past the gimmicks and the props . . . you can't hide from *Him* behind a poodle.

So, let's stop putting on the dog and get real. Let's start by developing the habit of genuine, transparent conversation. Let's admit to one another our failures and ask for prayer for specific needs and accountability between brothers and sisters in Christ.

The truth is the Christian experience should be a breeding ground for godly partnerships and persistent prayer . . . not for posing with lap dogs for pious portraits.

The church is simply no place for putting on the dog. Maybe we ought to hang a sign in the lobby that reminds us all: "No Poodles Allowed . . . Come Just as You Are."

Prayer Point: Maybe it's been awhile since you looked in the mirror of God's Word to see what you really look like. Perhaps there are still poodles in your own portrait that you need to pray for God's help to remove. Will you pray for God to reveal them to you today? Once He does, pray that He will give you courage to make the changes.

Extra Refreshment: Read Galatians 3, where Paul rebukes a group of Christians for putting on the dog of legalism.

Day 21 - Father Knows Best

Romans 8:28

And we know that God causes all things to work together for good to those who love God, to those who are called according to His purpose.

Have you ever volunteered to work in a nursery or preschool and noticed that toddlers never thank teachers for taking something away from them? When was the last time you heard a child say, "Hey, thanks, Teacher . . . it was about time I shared that Tonka Truck with somebody else." Or, "Thanks a lot for taking those Cheerios away from me . . . seems like I haven't been able to go anywhere without 'em lately!"

Hardly—it's the other way around, isn't it? Most times kids have a fit because they want *more* of something, not *less*.

I remember going to the grocery store one day to grab some fruit and vitamin-enhanced bottled water. Okay—I picked up a bag of chips and some donuts as well . . . my doctor said I needed a balanced diet!

While I was busy scouring the aisles, I noticed a mother who seemed rather worn. I quickly realized why. Her daughter [who looked to be about two years old] was standing up in the back of the grocery cart crying at the top of her lungs. This little red-haired girl was having a meltdown right there on Aisle 6.

What a sight! All blotchy-faced with tears streaming down her cheeks, she was standing on her tiptoes, her knuckles white as she held onto the side of the cart.

She was mad! In fact, if she had been bigger we would have all been in danger!

Despite the exhausting tantrum, I still remember her mother calmly saying over and over again, "No, you can't have that . . . no, you can't have that either . . . no . . . no . . . *no.*"

The little girl was too young to realize that her mother was actually protecting her. Pesticides, pills, and bottles of cleaning fluid aren't good packages to put in your mouth. But tell that to a two-year-old.

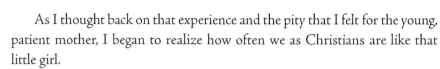

As I thought back on that experience and the pity that I felt for the young, patient mother, I began to realize how often we as Christians are like that little girl.

We might not always throw a fit—at least not externally—but how often do we reach for a relationship or a job or a dream and get frustrated with God when He says, "No . . . no . . . *no.*"

The truth is we're a lot more like that two-year-old on Aisle 6 than we'd like to admit. She saw things she wanted but didn't realize they were things she didn't need. All she knew was that big bottle of Windex looked like Kool-Aid but her mom wasn't letting her have a drink. And she was thirsty, for goodness' sake!

I wonder how many times our Father in heaven patiently listens to us fuss and fume, knowing we'll never come back to thank Him for saving us from something harmful.

How often do we go back to our Savior later in life and say, "Lord, thanks so much for protecting me from those things I wanted but certainly didn't need." Or "I was thirsty and thought that stuff would quench my thirst, but You knew better . . . so, thank You."

Are you having an internal tug-of-war with God right now over some object of your affection? Has He kept something just out of reach that you're convinced would be good for you? Has He refused to give you something you want—something, or someone, you'd rather not be without?

No matter what you might be going through, take time today to thank God for always being a loving Father—the Parent who has promised to provide for you what is good and best, even when it doesn't feel like it.

Prayer Point: Instead of fussing and fuming with the Lord today over some unrealized desire, quiet your heart in confidence as you thank Him for being the Perfect Parent—for withholding harmful and destructive things while offering good and perfect gifts that He knows will satisfy and sustain you.

Extra Refreshment: Read James 1.

Day 22 - Without Love
1 Corinthians 13:2

If I have the gift of prophecy, and know all mysteries and all knowledge; and if I have all faith, so as to remove mountains, but do not have love, I am nothing.

O f all the many kinds of "loves" in our world today, it fascinates me that when people see true love in action, they intuitively know it is the real thing.

I recently read a few statements from children regarding love, and some of them were rather profound.

+ Rebecca [age 8] said, "When my grandmother got arthritis, she couldn't bend down to paint her toenails anymore, so my grandfather does it for her. That's love."

+ Danny [age 7] said, "When my mommy makes coffee for my daddy and she takes a sip before giving it to him to make sure the taste is

+ Elaine [age 5] said, "Love is when Mommy gives Daddy the best piece of chicken." I like the way she thinks!

Most of these kids understand acts of sacrifice to be a reflection of *agape* love. But some of their companions missed the mark a little bit.

+ Like Karl who said, "Love is when a girl puts on perfume and a boy puts on shaving lotion and they go out and smell each other!"

+ Lauren said, "I know my older sister loves me because she gives me all her old clothes and has to go out and buy new ones." She'll catch on one day!

+ But Jessica perhaps delivered the most profound statement of all when she said, "You really shouldn't say 'I love you' unless you mean it. But if you mean it, you should say it a lot, because people forget."

In 1 Corinthians 13, Paul delivers to the church in Corinth one of the most remarkable, yet challenging pieces of prose on the subject of true love. In the process, he shatters the myths that abound today.

He effectively says, "It doesn't matter who you are, who you think you are, or who others think you are; if you sacrificially act toward others with *agape* love, your life will be meaningful."

That may seem hard to swallow at first, but when we test his statement in every aspect of life, we realize that he is right on the money.

Think about it: what is a marriage without love? Or a family? Or a friendship? Or a church? Or a career? Without love, life is like a fireplace without a fire or a pool without water. It's cold . . . it's empty.

The Bible makes it clear that "God is love." He doesn't just love or act in love or say He loves. He *is* love! And that means our ability to *agape*-love is a gift that comes directly from His character. When we love others, we are acting most like God, for that is who He is.

The tragedy in our world is not that people don't love—many do. Even unbelieving wives taste the coffee before handing it to their husbands; they even give them the best piece of chicken. They just don't know why.

Apart from God, the world not only loses the reason to love but has no incentive to continue to love someone when the recipient is unloving in return.

Love, at its core, grows cold and is empty if we do not surrender to the God of love Who is the source of *agape* love.

Let's take to heart this description from Paul and remind ourselves today that were it not for Christ's *agape* love toward us, we would not be able to offer it faithfully to others.

Demonstrating the character of Christ is *agape* love . . . it might include—but goes way beyond—giving away the best piece of chicken!

Prayer Point: As little Jessica so poignantly challenged us, let's take time today and prayerfully consider someone we can show love to in a substantial way. Then, thank God for the undeserved love He has given you in Christ. Ask Him to show you some tangible way that you can demonstrate His love to someone else.

Extra Refreshment: Read 1 Corinthians 13.

Day 23 - Best Friends Forever

John 15:15

"No longer do I call you slaves, for the slave does not know what his master is doing; but I have called you friends, for all things that I have heard from My Father I have made known to you.

A very special event happened some years ago on October 31. No, it wasn't Halloween, with thoughts of extra candy at hand. And it wasn't the "beginning" of the Protestant Reformation—for all you spiritually and historically minded people reading this.

It was something quite personal: the birth of our fourth child, Charity, occurred early on the morning of October 31.

She is our last child . . . *I promise.* She is the child of my "old age," as I often remind her.

As I was sifting through some old notes recently, I came across a story which told the beginning of a tradition that Charity and I still carry on to this day.

When she was around two-and-one-half years old, she could not pronounce her *r*'s. I remember her coming into our bedroom one evening with some of her favorite books and asking me to read them. She snuggled down beside me on a pillow and smiled really big as I opened to the first page. But before I began to read, she looked up at me and said, "You'*we* my best f*w*iend."

I have to admit she said the same thing to her mother as well, but she didn't mean it quite the same way as when she said it to me. You'll just have to trust me on that one!

A few days after that incident she went up to her mother and announced, "I'm gonna go see my f*w*iend named Daddy."

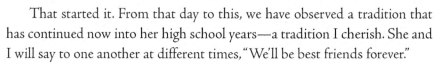

That started it. From that day to this, we have observed a tradition that has continued now into her high school years—a tradition I cherish. She and I will say to one another at different times, "We'll be best friends forever."

That's why whenever October 31 rolls around in the Davey household, nothing—not even a national party or an ecclesiastical event—can hold a candle to the celebration of my daughter and the reminder that we will be friends . . . forever.

As I began thinking of that sentimental little promise I share with Charity, I considered how God has so clearly given the same message to us throughout Scripture.

We are His children now—adopted through the finished work of His own beloved Son. And it doesn't end there as if salvation were nothing more than a cold theological transaction

It is much more personal. In fact, we are not just regenerated disciples of Christ but someone He considers His "friends."

Although Paul elsewhere will call himself a bond servant to Christ, as well as a slave to righteousness, he also reveals the remarkable truth that what ultimately defines our relationship to our Lord is everlasting friendship.

Let this thought warm your heart today with greater affection for Him. He is revealed as many things in Scripture: a consuming fire, the Lion of the Tribe of Judah, the Great Counselor, and a righteous Judge, among other titles.

But for those who have accepted Him by faith alone, He is something far more personal and intimate to us all: He is our friend.

In fact, we will be best friends . . . *forever*!

Prayer Point: As you open your Bible today, pull up a chair and imagine that you're sitting next to your best friend, eagerly awaiting the story He is about to read to you. Take time today to thank Him for being such a loving Friend who is always there for you.

Extra Refreshment: Read John 17, where Christ prays an intimate prayer to the Father, revealing the love that He has for you.

Day 24 - Dry Bones
Ecclesiastes 12:13

The conclusion, when all has been heard, is: fear God and keep His commandments, for this applies to every person.

In his book *Bones of Contention* [the leading creationist work in fossil study], Professor Marvin Lubenow tells the story of Sir Arthur Keith, one of the greatest anatomists of the twentieth century.

Arthur Keith [1866-1955] was a Scottish anatomist and anthropologist who became a fellow of theRoyal College of Surgeons of England. In 1908 Keith heard that bones had been found just forty miles from downtown London. After inspecting the bones himself, he considered them a monumental discovery. It was soon announced by the Geological Society of London that these were the remains of the earliest known Englishman, *Eoanthropus dawsoni*—otherwise known as the "Piltdown Man."

The bones quickly became the darling of the scientific culture and the personal obsession of Sir Arthur Keith. To him they were *the* validation of his evolutionary beliefs.

Over the course of his lifetime, Keith would write more on the subject of the Piltdown Man than anyone else. His most famous work, *The Antiquity of Man*, used the bones of the Piltdown Man to explain our human origins.

In 1953, however, science caught up with speculation, and the British Museum proclaimed the entire discovery a fraud. Their investigation undeniably shattered the myth of the bones as a missing link to prehistoric man.

The Piltdown Man was actually nothing more than the tampered- with remains from a human corpse. The bones had been treated with iron salts to make them appear old. Careful observations through microscopic lenses revealed scratch marks on the surface of the teeth—evidence that the teeth had been filed down to make them appear sharp.

Sir Arthur Keith was eighty-six years old when the fraud was discovered.

Some of his colleagues visited him at his home to break the difficult news to him. The bones which had captivated his entire adult life [his believing they

were evidence that discounted creation] had themselves been discovered to be a hoax.

His life's work—the foundation upon which he had based his speculation—was now meaningless. And he found out at the end of his life!

One man in Scripture who experienced something similar was King Solomon. As an old man, he looked back over his accomplishments and achievements. All his wealth, chariots, horses, gardens, buildings, and wives were now meaningless. He realized the only thing that really mattered in life was to fear God and keep His commandments. Nothing else would bring purpose and satisfaction to life.

As a young man, Arthur Keith attended evangelistic meetings in Edinburgh and Aberdeen and watched students make their commitment to Jesus Christ. He even claimed that during a few of those meetings he felt "on the verge of conversion." Instead, he chose to reject the Gospel because he thought it contradicted the truths of science.

The tragedy of Sir Arthur Keith and Solomon is that they are not alone. Men and women all over the world live their lives every day for what they *think* will bring them pleasure.

No matter where you are today—rich or poor, single or married, old or young—learn from the lives of two men who failed to live for what mattered.

Follow the advice of an aged Solomon who learned late in life: obey God's Word and live a life that respects and trusts His leadership.

This kind of lifestyle will never be meaningless. In fact, it is the only life that produces satisfaction . . . both now and forever.

Prayer Point: Give this day to the Lord in prayer and ask Him to guide all your steps—even the ones that seem insignificant—so that in the end, you won't have to look over your shoulder with regret.

Extra Refreshment: Read Ecclesiastes 12

Day 25 - You're on Candid Camera!

Ephesians 4:30

Do not grieve the Holy Spirit of God, by whom you were sealed for the day of redemption.

I received an unwanted surprise in the mail not long ago. At first I didn't understand why someone was sending me pictures of my Ford F-150, but it suddenly dawned on me that I had received a notice from the Cary Police Department.

My beloved town had installed cameras at key intersections that were designed to take photographs of drivers in the act of running red lights.

Doesn't technology just warm your heart?

It seems that I was one of those drivers . . . and I was looking at the proof! There were three photographs of my truck: the first, in the left turn lane; the second, in the middle of the intersection with the traffic signal above; the third [and the clincher], a close-up of my license plate—POIMENAS.

POIMENAS is the Greek word for *shepherds*, which is the same word translated *pastor* in the plural form. When I first got that special license plate, my wife told me she was glad it was in Greek because of the way I drive!

I didn't think that was funny.

The uniqueness of my license plate didn't help my cause any; there was no denying that this black Ford F-150 bearing a license plate with a foreign language definitely belonged to me. The town of Cary instructed me to send 50 dollars by mail or else face further civil action. In the face of such clear evidence, I immediately forked over the money.

I have to admit though it was really odd seeing pictures of me driving through an intersection while overhead [shown clearly in the photograph] the light was as red as Rudolph's nose.

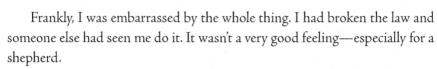

Frankly, I was embarrassed by the whole thing. I had broken the law and someone else had seen me do it. It wasn't a very good feeling—especially for a shepherd.

But that got me thinking: what if we were to go to our mailbox tomorrow and find a surprise letter filled with snapshots of all the things we had done the day before, including facial expressions and captions of the words we had spoken. I wonder how many of the photographs would bring us embarrassment or chagrin.

The Apostle Paul encourages us not to "grieve the Holy Spirit, by whom we have been sealed for the day of redemption."

The truth is, wherever we go we take God's Spirit with us. Whatever we say in private, He hears. Whatever thoughts we think that no one else can see, He sees. I imagine we must grieve Him often.

Unfortunately, we don't have the motivation to stop sinning because we see our sin caught on camera. Frankly, there aren't cameras powerful enough to capture the gossip, pride, and rebellion that can escape our lips and occupy our hearts every day. But God sees it all . . . and it grieves His heart.

So, let's start today by praying that God will open our eyes to see what He sees and give our hearts a sensitivity to even the smallest transgression that might otherwise slip by unnoticed.

Maybe it's not such a bad idea to pretend there's a camera following us . . . or should I say *dwelling* inside us!

Prayer Point: As you begin or end this day in God's Word, pray for God to give you an awareness of His abiding presence with you. Then pray as the Psalmist often prayed for God to give you clean hands and a pure heart.

Extra Refreshment: Read Psalm 139, taking special note of verses 22-24, as David prays for God to reveal those sins in his heart which he is not able to see.

Day 26 - Piercing the Darkness

Psalm 77:6

I will remember my song in the night . . .

Darkness is actually more than the absence of light. It is also a place—a place of fear, emptiness, and loneliness.

A Jewish man named Eliezer Wiesel experienced this darkness and wrote about it in his book, *Night*. He describes one of the most horrible chapters ever recorded in the history of mankind: the Holocaust.

As a teenager, Elie Wiesel was sent to the concentration camp at Auschwitz during Hitler's maddening reign; later he was moved to the camps at Buna, Buchenwald, and Gleiwitz. According to Elie's testimony, he had seen all the Jews in his village banded together, stripped of their possessions, and loaded into cattle cars.

He saw his mother, little sister, and all his family disappear into an oven fueled with human flesh. He saw children hanged and weak men killed by fellow prisoners for a piece of bread.

Wiesel wrote of the night the train in which he was riding pulled up at the camp. Coils of ominous black smoke billowed from the tower; beneath it lay the ovens. For the first time in his life, Elie smelled the scent of burning human flesh. He wrote:

> Never shall I forget that night, seven times cursed. Never shall I forget that smoke. Never shall I forget the little faces of the children whose bodies I saw turned into wreaths of smoke beneath a silent blue sky. Never shall I forget that silence which deprived me, for all eternity, of the desire to live. Never shall I forget those moments which murdered my God and my soul and turned my dreams to dust.

That night was dark for Elie Wiesel and many other Jews, but the greater tragedy is that the darkness found its way into Elie's heart. Not only did he watch friends and family die on that fateful night, but he claims that his God died as well.

But there was another person who entered that same dark night; she came forth as a shining light. Her name was Corrie ten Boom. Although she herself was not a Jew, she and her family had been discovered aiding Jews and had been sent to one of the German death camps as well. She, too, saw people murdered, watched her own sister Betsie die from illness in the camp, and felt the gnaw of hunger and the sting of the whip.

But in her account of the terrible things which transpired all around her, there was a thread of hope. She wrote of the Bible study that some of the Jews held in secret, of the hymn singing, and of the many acts of compassion and sacrifice they offered to one another.

Throughout her days of blackness, Corrie continued to trust in a God who was at work even in a cave as dark as hers! She would later write, "I discovered that there is not a pit where God's love is not deeper still!"

Corrie ten Boom could relate to the author of Psalm 77:6; he, too, found himself in a dark, empty place where God seemed distant. But as the darkness deepened, the volume of his song increased. He committed to singing in the middle of his long, dark night.

The same is true for us. The darker the night grows, the more we see God's light shining around us—if we're willing to look with the eyes of faith and trust.

That is a choice we have to make. Either we can collapse in our discouragement and give up on God as Elie Wiesel did, or we can praise Him in the midst of it, as did Corrie ten Boom.

Are you experiencing darkness right now in your own life? Does God seem distant and the heavens made of brass? Let me encourage you to look farther ahead by faith . . . the faithful light of Christ is inviting you to take just one more step in His direction.

Every act of trust and every offering of praise are stubborn refusals to give in to the darkness; they are faith-filled decisions to walk in the light.

Stay the course . . . and don't forget to sing in the dark.

Prayer Point: Take time to ask God to help you remember that when the darkness comes, His light is ever present. Thank Him for the times when He led you out of the dark.

Extra Refreshment: Read again all of Psalm 23 to remember that the Good Shepherd is with us . . . even in the valley.

Day 27 - Deposits and Investments

2 Timothy 2:2

The things which you have heard from me . . . entrust these to faithful men who will be able to teach others also.

Isn't it interesting that Jesus Christ never said to make disciples by taking them to church—or to a Bible study group, for that matter. Not that these activities aren't an integral part of a disciple's growth, but the Lord has something much more personal in mind.

My life was personally impacted in such a way by a college professor. He had taught my father thirty-five years before I was enrolled in his class at the Bible college. For my entire college career, Dr. Fred Afman called me by my father's name. I never bothered to tell him my name wasn't Keith!

There were times I'd read something in Scripture that confused me or hear a preacher say something in Chapel that troubled me, and I would go to this older gentleman's office for advice. He'd answer his door, smile, and say, "Well, hello there, Keith; come on in and have a seat." There in his office he would answer my questions, or even correct what I'd heard in Chapel, from Scripture.

This same life-on-life investment continued in seminary. I often went to Dr. Eugene Petersen's office, where he would answer my many questions about ministry, pastoring, and preaching. With patience and care he addressed my thoughts and corrected any misconceptions. His personal investment fanned my desire for pastoring and preaching the Word of God; it grew into a steady flame.

I will forever be indebted to these two men. They modeled our verse for today as they modeled life-on-life mentoring.

That word *entrust* was a first-century banking term that literally meant "to make a deposit." Paul is saying in our text, "You have learned things from me, Timothy; now I want you to take that truth and personally deposit it into the lives of other disciples."

When you teach a child something about Christ, you are making a deposit into his heart; when you share Scripture or prayer with another believer, you are making a life-on-life deposit that Christ would define as true discipleship.

Frankly, my writing at this very moment reflects what I've had modeled and taught to me by others. That's what discipleship is . . . taking what Jesus Christ taught us and depositing it into the lives of other believers.

There are three components that define true discipleship. The first is *touch*. You can't disciple at a distance. The only way iron can sharpen iron is through personal connection. This is the touch that invests when others withdraw; it perseveres when others disappear.

Second, you must make the commitment of *time*. You won't be able to reproduce your life and passion for Christ in a day. You didn't grow overnight—we humans aren't like Jack's beanstalk! We're more like apple trees that need a lot of time to grow before fruit begins to appear.

The third component is *truth*: the truth of God's Word. This keeps the discipleship process on track, rather than one opinion contradicting another. Without truth, discipleship of any kind—coaching a team, tutoring a student, teaching an instrument—will not have permanence. The center of spiritual discipleship is the truth of Scripture.

The goal is more than information . . . it's *transformation*.

If you know the Lord Jesus Christ as your Savior, you have all three of these qualities at your disposal.

Is there someone in your life in need of a deposit—an investment that will last for eternity? Then act . . . begin a life-on-life influence, no matter how small or simple. Offer a personal touch, an investment of your time, and the principles of God's truth.

That kind of investment will reproduce fruit well beyond your lifetime. In light of eternity, make a deposit into someone's life . . . *today!*

Prayer Point: Ask the Lord to show you one person with whom you can start rubbing shoulders today. Perhaps you need to ask Him to help you find someone to disciple you. Ask Him to give you the humility and confidence you need to be involved in "life rubbing against life" as you grow more into the likeness of Jesus.

Extra Refreshment: Read John 1:35-42 and notice the investment made by Andrew. Who knew his influence would produce such abundant fruit?!

Day 28 - Skeletons in the Closet

1 Corinthians 2:5

So that your faith would not rest on the wisdom of men, but on the power of God.

When God decided to give mankind the record of Scripture, He accomplished it by giving a record of people's lives. Strangely enough, He decided not to edit out all the failures of our forefathers or the sins of the saints.

One wealthy media mogul commented not too long ago that "Christians are losers." What he probably meant was that all of the Christians he had come in contact with had been less successful than he had been. Then again, he might have known a Christian or two who had failed to live up to what he intuitively knew a Christian should be.

Frankly, you'd think that God would do everything possible to enhance the reputation of His saints—not spill the beans on what they were like during moments of total failure and rebellion.

However, one of the strongest arguments for the inspiration of Scripture is that it includes details that you and I probably would have edited out . . . or covered up. But God didn't. He pulled the skeletons out of the closet of some of His choicest servants. He recorded their failures, often with more detail than their successes.

God could have left the flawless history of Abraham intact. After all, he was called one of God's friends. Did we need to know that Abraham lied about his wife being his sister in order to save his own skin—not once, but twice?! And then we learned that his son Isaac would inherit the same problem of not telling the truth—too much information?

And what about King David? We would have liked to hear only that David was a man after God's own heart, he courageously killed Goliath, served as Israel's greatest king, and prepared Solomon to build the great temple. Did

God really have to tell us of David's adultery and murderous cover-up . . . and then throw in the account about his utter failure as a father to Absalom?

Then there's Jonah. The summation of his ministry could have ended with chapter three, where all of Nineveh repents after hearing him preach. Now that's a success story worth repeating! Instead, God tacks on one more chapter which shows Jonah throwing a temper tantrum because he wanted Nineveh to *burn*, not turn. At the end of his biography we find out that Jonah wasn't interested in their redemption, but their annihilation.

Why scuff the polish on the shoes of our greatest saints? The answer is equally straightforward: God wants to communicate that He uses undeserving, foolish, sinful, faithless, and even incompetent people to accomplish His work in the world . . . which leaves room for you and me.

The fuller story of these biographies in Scripture reveals a God of incredible grace and compassion (not to mention *patience*), Who uses frail, stumbling children to fulfill His purposes.

He's also letting us know that failures aren't fatal. Where sin abounds, grace abounds even more.

If you've failed in your past [think: Abraham, Moses, David, Samuel, Gideon, Peter, Mark, and the list goes on], you're in good company. Get on your knees and confess your sin, and then get back up on your feet and live for Christ.

Add your biography of faith to all the others of past and present generations. Delight in the fact that God has the gracious habit of using losers to demonstrate His ultimate victory over sin and sorrow.

So shove those skeletons back into the closet, lock the door, and get into the game . . . you have no excuse to sit this one out!

Prayer Point: Ask the Lord to help you remember that He alone is able, trustworthy, and good. Thank Him for these truths and reflect before Him on the many times that He has forgiven you in your life. Thank Him for second, third, fourth (and even more!) chances to serve Him.

Extra Refreshment: Read Matthew chapter 1 and note the names of and references to former failures.

Day 29 - Redeeming the Years

James 4:14

You do not know what your life will be like tomorrow. You are just a vapor that appears for a little while and then vanishes away.

Do you realize that the only time in our lives when we liked growing older was when we were kids?

When you were less than 10 years old, you were so excited about aging that you used fractions. If someone asked you how old you were, you responded, "I'm five . . . and one-half!"

Then you hit double-digits and began dreaming of the next major milestone: 13. Oh, to be a teenager . . . *life will finally be all that I dreamed it would be*. Or so we thought.

When 13 finally got there, you immediately began skipping years. If someone asked how old you were, you said, "I'm almost 16." You might have two years to go, but that's completely ignored. You were *almost* 16.

Then 21 came and you'd really arrived—right? Even the words sounded like a ceremony: you became 21! But that didn't last very long, did it? Soon you turned 30 and wondered where the time went!

Next thing you know, you're pushing 40, and not long after, you reach 50.

Strange how we word this progression of time, isn't it? You *become* 21, *turn* 30, you're *pushing* 40, *reach* 50, and you *make it* to 60! By then you've built up so much momentum that you *hit* 70!

After that you're simply "in your 80s." But if you make it past that, you start going backward! You say, "I was just 92," or, "I was 95 last year."

Then a really strange phenomenon occurs: if you're one of the select few who make it to the century mark, you start thinking like a kid again. Someone asks how old you are and you say, "I'm one hundred and one-half . . . I'm *almost* 102!"

It doesn't matter where you find yourself on this timeline, time flies for all of us. Tomorrows seem like they will never come, and yesterdays seem like they never happened. The psalmist writes in 103:15:

As for man, his days are like grass; as a flower of the field, so he flourishes. When the wind has passed over it, it is no more, and its place acknowledges it no longer.

It really doesn't matter what age you are. Whether you're 24 or 84, the question is: what are you doing with the time you have *left*? How are you spending your life *now*?

If we were cats, we might get nine chances at life (so the saying goes) but as it stands, we only get one. Just one chance at however life unfolds in God's sovereign plan to be: a loving spouse; a godly parent; a faithful friend; a good servant of Jesus Christ.

So let's take the words of Ephesians 5:16 to heart and "make the most of our time."

Be careful not to measure your life by birthdays or special occasions alone; evaluate it by what God is accomplishing in and through the energy and efforts of your life.

When I was a boy, my parents had a plaque hanging over their dining room door that read,

> Only one life, 'twill soon be past;
> Only what's done for Christ will last.

That's a good reminder. Life is about much more than aging—it's about living . . . living every moment for the glory of God.

Prayer Point: Ask the Lord to help you make some changes or develop some disciplines to enable you to capture the most of your time—right now—for His glory. Ask God to prepare you with His will in mind, trusting Him that when it does not match your plans, His ways are always perfect.

Extra Refreshment: Read all of Psalm 103 for a bit more perspective.

Day 30 - Rekindling the Flame

1 Thessalonians 1:6

You also became imitators of us and of the Lord, having received the word in much tribulation with the joy of the Holy Spirit.

In my study at home I have a small, yellowed piece of paper framed in glass. It was given to me by a missionary who works with Chinese believers.

Today, millions of Chinese Christians are meeting secretly in house churches to study the Word of God together. Many of them do not have a personal copy of the Bible. Often entire churches do not have access to a complete copy of the Scriptures.

That is why this old piece of paper is so special to me; it happens to be a handwritten page—a portion of the New Testament in the Mandarin language. This piece of paper was once someone's copy of Scripture.

Imagine . . . they didn't have a Bible—they had a *page*.

Much like the Thessalonians, these believers obviously hungered to hear and have the Word of God. They had no doubt copied it many times over so that other believers could read from God's Word, perhaps never before hearing the truths that were written on this small page.

What a contrast to most of us! The Evangelical Christian Publishers Association estimates that the average church-going family in America owns at least four Bibles.

Perhaps one reason that we don't treasure the Scriptures is because we have such ready access to them. It's easy to take precious things for granted. We may have copies of the Bible lying on tables, closet shelves, and bookcases but this can lead to a serious problem: how does the truth within the pages of that closed Book penetrate our lives?

There is a vast difference between having the Bible inside our home and having the Bible inside our heart.

In 1 Thessalonians 1:6, we are told that the believers received the Word of God. They readily received its truth, even though it would mean tribulation and persecution.

What we take for granted, the early church received with great hunger, as does the Chinese church today.

We conclude these 30 days of contemplation with this challenge: let's ask Christ to rekindle in our hearts a greater love for His Word and a greater desire to hear and study it.

Oh, that He would imprint on our hearts what we hold in our hands!

God does not want you to simply possess a Bible . . . He wants the Bible to possess *you.*

Prayer Point: Ask God to give you a stronger passion for His Word. That is exactly what we need: a hunger and thirst for the written Word—which leads to a greater love for Jesus Christ, the Living Word.

Extra Refreshment: Read all of Psalm 119 and take note of each verse delivering some truth or principle about the Word of God.

Scripture Index

Printed in Great Britain
by Amazon

24645324R00037